EXTREME ANIMALS

MARVELOUS MAMMALS

Isabel Thomas

Raintree

Chicago, Illinois

www.capstonepub.com
Visit our website to find out more information about Heinemann-Raintree books.

To order:
☎ Phone 800-747-4992
💻 Visit www.capstonepub.com
to browse our catalog and order online.

Edited by Daniel Nunn, John-Paul Wilkins, and Rebecca Rissman
Designed by Philippa Jenkins
Picture research by Elizabeth Alexander
Production by Victoria Fitzgerald

Originated by Capstone Global Library
Printed and bound in China by CTPS

16 15 14 13 12
10 9 8 7 6 5 4 3 2 1

Library of Congress Cataloging-in-Publication Data

Cataloging-in-Publication data is on file at the Library of Congress.

ISBN:

978-1-4109-4681-2 (HC) 978-1-4109-4687-4 (PB)

Acknowledgments

We would like to thank the following for permission to reproduce photographs: Alamy p. 4 (© Michael Patrick O'Neill); Corbis pp. 16, 17 (© Ken Catania/Visuals Unlimited); FLPA pp. 15 (© Mandal Ranjit), 18 (Michael & Patricia Fogden/Minden Pictures); Getty Images pp. 8 (Danita Delimont/Gallo Images), 12 (Martin Harvey/Gallo Images), 14 (Nigel Dennis/Gallo Images), 23 (Kevin Schafer/Stone); iStockphoto pp. 11 (© YinYang), 26 (© steve greer); Nature Picture Library pp. 13 (© Dave Watts), 27 (© Edwin Giesbers); Photolibrary pp. 6 (Tim Jackson/OSF), 7 (Ed Reschke/Peter Arnold Images), 19 (Maurice Tibbles/OSF), 21 (Tom Brakefield/White), 24 (Thomas Haider/OSF), 25 (Brigitte Marcon/Bios); Shutterstock pp. 5 (© Cheryl Ann Quigley), 9 (© Anke van Wyk), 10 (© Noo), 20 (© enciktat), 22 (© Lukich).

Main cover photograph of Bactrian camel reproduced with permission of Shutterstock (© argonaut). Background cover photograph of leopard print reproduced with permission of Shutterstock (© WitR).

Every effort has been made to contact copyright holders of material reproduced in this book. Any omissions will be rectified in subsequent printings if notice is given to the publisher.

Disclaimer

All the Internet addresses (URLs) given in this book were valid at the time of going to press. However, due to the dynamic nature of the Internet, some addresses may have changed, or sites may have changed or ceased to exist since publication. While the author and publisher regret any inconvenience this may cause readers, no responsibility for any such changes can be accepted by either the author or the publisher.

Some words are shown in bold, **like this**. You can find out what they mean by looking in the glossary.

Contents

Extreme Mammals. 4

Prickly Porcupines 6

Nosy Elephants 8

Crafty Camels 10

Bizarre Bills 12

Animal Armor. 14

Touchy-Feely Moles 16

Flapping Fingers 18

Terrible Tigers 20

Bright Blue Bottoms! 22

Whale of a Noise 24

Mighty Munchers. 26

Record-Breakers. 28

Glossary. 30

Find Out More 31

Index 32

Extreme Mammals

Do you think you know everything about mammals? Think again! All mammals have hair or fur, and they feed their babies with milk. But the differences between mammals are what make them **extreme**.

Most mammals live on land. A few live in the ocean, like this dugong.

Some mammals have strange bodies. Some behave in weird ways. These features help them find **mates** or food— or avoid getting eaten themselves!

Prickly Porcupines

Porcupines have **extreme** fur. Each of their **spines** is a giant, stiff hair. When a porcupine is scared, it raises and rattles its spines. It does this using the same muscles that give people goose bumps.

porcupine

If the **predator** doesn't run away, the porcupine has another trick. It runs backward and pushes its prickly bottom into the attacker's face!

Nosy Elephants

An elephant's trunk is an amazing tool. Elephants use them to:

- grab food
- suck up water to drink or wash
- **snorkel** underwater
- smell and breathe
- figure out where other elephants are
- trumpet.

tusk

trunk

African elephants are the largest land mammals in the world.

Crafty Camels

Bactrian camels survive in rocky deserts. There is little to eat and drink. The camel's lip collects snot that trickles out of its nose. The snot flows back into the camel's mouth, so no water is wasted!

humps store fat for energy

Camels swallow their food whole. Then they throw it up and chew it again to make it softer! This helps them **digest** very tough foods. Camels have eaten bones, rope, and even tents!

Bizarre Bills

Platypuses have soft, rubbery **bills**. Bills help these weird mammals to sense food. Using its bill, a platypus can hunt underwater with its eyes closed.

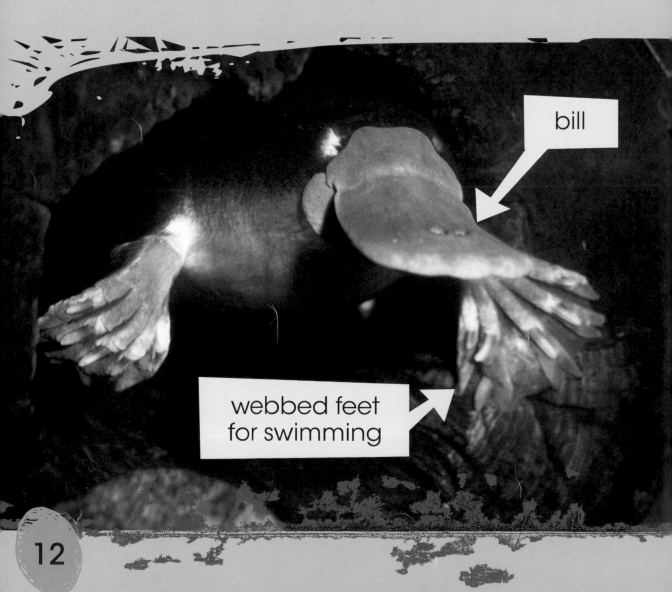

bill

webbed feet for swimming

DID YOU KNOW?

Platypuses lay eggs, like reptiles. But their babies drink milk from their mothers, like other mammals. Milk oozes out of the mother's skin. The babies lick it off her fur.

Animal Armor

A pangolin's body is covered in horny **scales** made from the same material as fingernails. When a pangolin is frightened, it rolls in a ball and flips the scales out like blades.

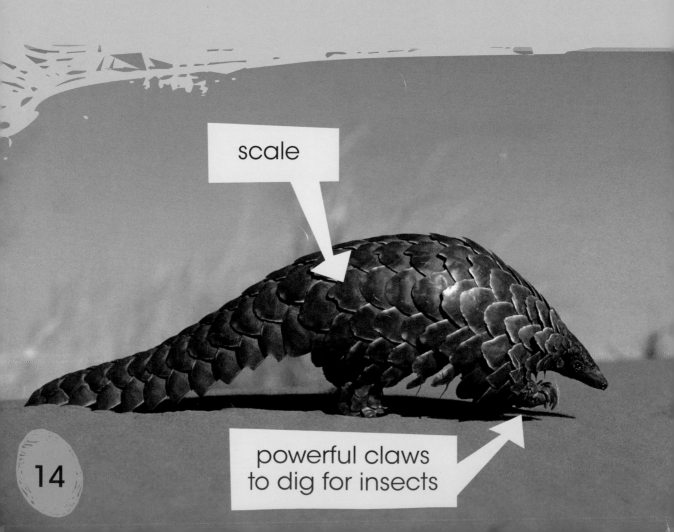

scale

powerful claws
to dig for insects

14

DID YOU KNOW?
Some pangolins can squirt a stinky liquid from their bottoms. It smells so disgusting it can scare away tigers!

Touchy-Feely Moles

The star-nosed mole lives in dark underground tunnels. It explores the world through its nose. Weird tentacles around its nose give it the best sense of touch of any mammal.

huge claws for digging

tentacles

How good is your sense of touch? Close your eyes and see how long it takes you to figure out what 12 objects are by touching them. It takes the star-nosed mole one second!

Flapping Fingers

Bats are the only mammals that can fly. Their wings are actually skin stretched between very long fingers. Bats also have amazing hearing. Some bats can hear the sound of an insect walking on a leaf!

Terrible Tigers

Tigers are the largest cats in the world. They are killing machines. Every part of their body is **adapted** for hunting meat. They can tackle enormous oxen and buffalo.

striped coat for **camouflage**

long teeth for a deadly bite

DID YOU KNOW?
A tiger's stripes are like a human fingerprint. No two tigers have the same pattern.

Bright Blue Bottoms!

How do you spot the most important people in your school? Mandrills show who is boss by turning their bottoms bright blue and red! They are the most colorful mammals.

The strongest, most feared males have the brightest bottoms.

long teeth
for fighting

orange beard

23

Whale of a Noise

Sperm whales make the loudest sound of any animal. Their booming clicks are as loud as a space rocket taking off. The sounds bounce off squid and fish. The **echo** tells the whale what and where the food is.

Mighty Munchers

A rodent's teeth never stop growing! This means they can chew through very hard things. Beavers can chomp through tree trunks. Rats can chew through lead and aluminum. Their teeth get damaged, but they quickly grow back.

beaver

DID YOU KNOW?

A rat's teeth grow 4 inches every year. If the rat cannot find anything to **gnaw**, its teeth will grow through its skull.

Record-Breakers

Which mammal do you think is the most **extreme**? Why? Take a look at some of these record-breaking mammals to help you decide.

What? Blue whale

Why? World's largest animal

Wow! Blue whales can grow to about 100 feet long. Even their babies weigh 2 to 3 tons. That is as much as a car!

What? Cheetah

Why? World's fastest land animal

Wow! Cheetahs can reach top speeds of 54 miles per hour. That is as fast as a speeding car!

What? Spotted hyena

Why? Best at clearing their plate

Wow! Strong jaws and teeth mean these **scavengers** can eat bones, skin, hooves, and horns!

What? Rhinoceros

Why? World's thickest skin

Wow! The skin on a rhino's back can be 1 inch thick, which is about the length of a paperclip.

What? Giraffe

Why? Tallest animal

Wow! Males can grow up to 20 feet tall—or three times taller than a door!

What? Three-toed sloth

Why? World's slowest mammal

Wow! This mammal moves at 0.15 miles per hour. That is only five times faster than a snail!

Glossary

adapted changed over time to become suited for a special purpose

bill hard mouth-part of a bird or other animal

camouflage colors or markings that help an animal to blend in with the things around it

echo sound caused by another sound bouncing off something

extreme unusual, amazing, or different from normal

digest break down food so that the body can use it

gnaw bite or chew on again and again

mate animal that can have babies together with another animal

predator animal that hunts other animals for food

scale horny or bony plate that overlaps with other plates to cover some animals' bodies

scavenger animal that finds and eats dead animals

snorkel tube that an animal uses to breathe through when its head is underwater

spine sharp, pointed body part that sticks out on some animals

Find Out More

Books

Meinking, Mary. *Crocodile vs. Wildebeest* (Predator vs. Prey). Chicago: Raintree, 2011.

Snedden, Robert. *Mammals* (Living Things). Mankato, Minn.: Smart Apple Media, 2008.

Solway, Andrew. *Killer Cats* (Wild Predators). Chicago: Heinemann Library, 2005.

Web sites

Learn more about mammals at this web site:
kids.discovery.com/tell-me/animals/mammals

Watch videos of marvelous mammals and other animals at this web site:
kids.nationalgeographic.com/kids/animals

Find facts, photos, and more about small mammals at this web site:
nationalzoo.si.edu/animals/smallmammals/forkids/default.cfm

Index

babies 4, 13, 28
Bactrian camels 10–11
bats 18–19
beavers 26
blue whales 28
bumblebee bats 19

cheetahs 28
claws 14, 16

dugongs 4

elephants 8–9

food 5, 8, 11, 12, 24, 25

giraffes 29

mandrills 22–23

pangolins 14–15
platypuses 12–13

porcupines 6–7
predators 7

rats 26, 27
rhinoceroses 29
right whales 25
rodents 26–27

scales 14
scavengers 29
sperm whales 24
spines 6, 7
spotted hyenas 29
star-nosed moles 16–17

teeth 20, 23, 26, 27, 29
three-toed sloths 29
tigers 15, 20–21
touch, sense of 16, 17

whales 24–25, 28